Just Human

Poetry by Abby Land

ISBN: 979-8-218-34610-2

DEDICATION

This collection is dedicated to my closest friends who nudged me to share my soul with the world. Without you, I would likely hold my feelings within. Thank you for being real, true, loyal, and accepting me even in my dramatic ways and messiness.

I love you all.

Just Human

Dear reader,

This book contains a lot of deep emotions. We go through mental health topics and topics of loss that might be things you have experienced or felt similarly to. Although some poems may be sad, there are always poems of resolution and healing. As someone who works in the mental health field, I know how important it is to acknowledge all emotions, including the ones that hurt or are uncomfortable. I wanted to mention some of these poems are from my own experience and many I have written through the lens of those around me such as, friends, strangers, or stories I have heard. I hope whether you have read poetry before, or if this is your first-time giving poetry a try, you find a favorite and can appreciate the beauty of mine and other's stories.

Love, Abs

Just Human

CONTENTS

Just Human

INSPIRED BY:

This book was inspired by many people, places, and things. This book includes poems full of hurt, sorrow, stories that are not mine, and love. I want to thank those who have been close to me for any amount of time, as some of these poems may be about you. Something I tell myself is, “I don’t have regrets because everything I’ve done and experienced, whether good or bad, has made me who I am today.” This book is inspired by the human experience, and I hope you can acknowledged the things that make us all just human.

Just Human

PART 1 : MENTAL HEALTH

Just Human

There is nothing like humanity
It is complex, intriguing, and bare
It seems the one who created it mastered insanity
Making our thoughts and emotions all there

But there is beauty in this chaos
We are so different from the other
But we all laugh, cry, and feel loss
We have something beautiful together
We are all just human

Out of Anxiety

In this moment I realized how fresh the air is
I looked and I found the sun again
Noticing all the little things
My laugh the dumb stuff brings

My eyes are now colored
There are seconds to be found
Telling the truth to go deeper
This choice may be dangerous, steeper

Taking short breaths
To live in the moment
I risk it all for the one chance
To slow my thoughts like a dance

I am now coming up
Going out and above
I am floating in the air
Not even the wind will make a tear

Learned Boundaries

I've finally learned my lessons
I've learned how to say "no"
I had a hard time in the past
But because it's so hard to let go

I'm not your leftovers or trash
And I shouldn't be thrown away
But since you really don't see that
There's no point in me to stay

I know who I am now
And I won't be treated less
Cause I know I'm a strong woman
That doesn't deserve your mess

I've worked hard for all I have
This time words can't tear me down
Becausc I finally found the strength
I'll never return to this town

Small Words are Large

I'll never forget the words you said
To me that lonesome day
Scarred on my brain, tattooed in my memory
We can never make words go away

I wished so badly I could unhear it
Wish I could have zipped up my ears
Because although you apologized
Your words are knit forever in those tears

I know how you feel now
But what knowledge have you gained
To be so close but so distant in spirit
I see neglect on your skin, it's stained

What I Can Control

I don't have any answers
But I know I'm trying my best

I don't know what is the solution
But I know I'll do good with rest

I don't know how to fix the problem
But I'll surround with the people who care

I don't know how to resolve the issue
But I know not getting through it is rare

I don't seem to have all the answers
But I do have some control
of the things I can do to function
And one day again I'll be whole

This is Called Healing

Being stuck in the mud
Trying to get clean
But I keep falling in
Can't handle the struggle
It is hopeless at times
But know there is an option

Maybe others can help
Some do and some don't
Some pull you a little out
Some shove you back down
Into the mud like before

But sit in the mud
Embrace the smell
Learn it's intricacies and war
Close your eyes and
Pause, remember you
This is what a plan's for

Found rocks in the mud
Push with my legs
Oh, I am so tired
Getting closer I think
I'm almost out
Hard work is required

I'm Out of the mud
But scratched up from it
One cannot forget this feeling
Although it still happened
Made it out of the mud
And this is what I call healing

Growing Pains

I have changed a lot I know
I look at my old self and I see
The progress that was slow
The mistakes I made are part of me
They're growing pains though

Everything I have gone through
And everyone who left
Became lessons that were new
And they taught me step by step
The growing pains were due

Although it was quite painful
And the end of it I didn't see
I've grown and I am grateful
Because all those pains made me
These are growing pains you see

Content

Not moving, just still
But looking at the waves
No storm, it's calm
Peace is all I crave

No worries, no stress
As I look left to right
No problems at all
This is living right

No movement or steps
This way I am content
Just air and just breeze
This is all that I dreamt

If I Grew Up Like You

If I grew up like you
I'd cry when I was a kid
And get yelled at when I did
Telling me to "be a man"

If I grew up like you
I wouldn't know who to trust
But knew that I just must
Be the man and provide

If I grew up like you
I'd never let a feeling show
Except anger when I hear "no"
And lose all control

If I grew up like you
I would be insecure
Push away people that ensure
I am good enough

Self-Doubt

You capture everyone you meet
But you doubt yourself

Every time they hold up the mirror
You close your eyes

Your world needs saving from the villain
But he is also you

You constantly sulk in your failure
Yet you've never failed at all

I Choose to Let Go

My choice is to drop that moment
I'm choosing to unhold its hand
To allow the feelings that came to go
Let them sink in the sand

To move on from this big event
And focus on much more
To embrace life and all its beauty
And the things there are to adore

I can't undo what happened
But I choose to loosen its hold
To look out the window and sleep at night
I know this strength is bold

Although it brought discomfort
The moment needed me there to be right
And now that I choose to let it go
I will be able to sleep alone at night

Loss

Rip out my heart
Or I'll do it myself
Disconnect my brain
My thoughts are concerning
Tell me it's a nightmare
And it will all be fixed tomorrow
My hope is too high
I can't lose you forever
Come back to me please
So I can breathe again

Hold Myself

You said get over it
It's what adults do
Don't give anyone a chance
To feel sorry for you

I held myself and you'll hold you too
Don't lean on anyone
That's what weak people do

But would you say that to her?
Yourself when you were younger
The times, you cried, and cried, and cried, and became so numb

Do you think if she would've had some support, she would've gone a different way?
She would've made different choices, not like one she still regrets today

Sure, you have a great life now but pushing away those who need you to care won't keep your life stable; It will keep it lonely and bare

Mental Illness

Some people will never understand
what I go through each day
that I can barely lift a hand

Some people never want to see
how I function so different
no, you aren't like me

Some people always talk
about how I am lazy,
or simply not enough

Some people don't know
I barely get up some days
And at times, I move slow

Some people will never see
I have a mental illness
and the illness has me

Overwhelm

I think I forgot to breathe
Do I even know how
My tears are falling like streams
Flooding my brain and now

Everything keeps happening
I have too many things to hold
Oh no now they're dropping
Like glass breaking in my soul

My head is now pounding
It doesn't like it when I cry
The thoughts they keep hounding
I'm okay, again I lie

How do I keep me together
When I'm strangled by the chaos
What happened to my normal
Someone help, I am so lost

Stop Saying Sorry

I'm tired of saying sorry for the feelings I expressed
For the moments I was down
And the things that went unsaid

I'm tired of saying sorry when you were the one at fault
I'm going to watch my words more
And put my sorry to halt

Pleasing people is a habit that needs to be put to rest
Because I've learned what I need
Sometimes myself first is best

Sometimes I Cry

I look fine on the outside, but sometimes I still cry
I remember all the hurt I went through that year
How I had great friends and then they abandoned me
But mainly how I felt completely alone
Sometimes I still cry to get out the emotion
And out of my head
To pull out the triggers and place them behind something I won't find for a while
But when I see them, I still cry
And maybe not in the moment, but when I'm by myself
Because I don't want people to think I'm not over it and not strong
I think of how some of the closest people were the worst support
But I love them regardless even when they didn't know how to love me in my pain

And though the tears come so few now, the laughter is addicting
I can smile at my cat, stare at the sky, and just breathe again
I sing loudly with my friends in the car with no worry in sight
Sometimes I laugh too hard I choke on my humorous thoughts
I can build others up and not be so sad
And I laugh and enjoy the dumbest things every day
Even though I sometimes cry

You Choose

It's a difficult thing for one to do
Choose decisions for them or make choices for you

It's a challenge that most people see
Do I follow along or make myself happy

Do I go along with what they think is right
Do I even get a thought, a say, or a fight

I believe decisions should be sacred and safe
Where other's opinions are not in their space

Ultimately, you'll be happier if you do
Make decisions for yourself and be authentic to you

Mad

I'm just mad

Mad at how nothing has worked out though I try my hardest
Mad that I don't receive what I give to others
Mad that you leave me feeling confused when I so clearly love you
Mad that even when I know I deserve more
I still stay

Too Heavy

Somethings are too heavy for me to bare
I feel like I'm carrying bricks down the stairs

Fixing everyone's problems and my own too
Don't you see this is nearly impossible to do

I would try and make everyone happy, but you'll see
That was the worst way, unbalanced, not me

But I'm trying to do what works and it's new
Your expectations are yours, and not mine to do

The news, stories, and work is so hard to see
Can't I just have one space that's only for me

It's Not Fair

It's not fair that everyone's life keeps going
and mine feels like it's stopped

Stopped and I'm stuck in cement
With no brain to decide what is next

My body is empty, I'm just a case
That feels the most intense emotions

Emotions that bounce around inside
Not landing at all, just constant

This is for Every Person who has Lost Someone

My stomach drops and I feel intense pain
My brain is fuzzy, and I can't even explain
Tears streaming down it should be expected
Balled up like paper never again perfected
My life has now changed to something intense
The loss I just bore, it is forever immense
They are gone in an instant, but here for a while
So hold loved ones close, laugh, dance, and smile
I watch now from above, my time on earth is done
It is seldom to realize both people lost someone.
This is for every person who has lost someone

Body

I want to cry every day when I see what I hate
I want to change but I know this is how my fate goes

I tell myself I'm no good with comparison the bully
I lie through my teeth trying so hard not to eat

I've considered it all, but I never fully commit
The fakeness I live in a mask called confidence

I don't see a change and it makes me only sicker
It's so bad to think, I'd be happy if I was thinner

Logic

Logic might be the death of me
Some say it's good some say overthinking
I will always weigh pros and cons
But in my brain my thoughts are sinking

Outside the box but before any trouble
I've thought of it all, not once but double
I like my logic it helps me see
The things of life I won't let control me

Emotional Dysregulation

Explosions all over my mind
Waiting for the time to go bye
Take a breath in hope it will flee
The anger is taking over me

Racing, jumping from place to place
Stare at one thing, stay in one space
No focus for a second or bit
Thinking of everything, all of it

Drowning in pools for sorrows of me
My head it hurts, and it is pounding
Wiping the tears until it's dry
Don't worry, 20 minutes and back to cry

Slower than slow and slow as can be
Like looking at it but I cannot see
Oh no how the time goes by
Goal not met, again I sigh

Overwhelmed with emotions and now I see
My emotions they now regulate me

Guardian Angel Saving You

Don't jump please don't
Just talk to me instead
If you do it she'll wake
And cause trouble in her head

Let's take off our shoes
We can just sleep it away
Let's change our mind, please
No decision like this today

I promise I'll make you happy
If you stay safe tonight
Because it's not fair if you do it
And make her too have to fight

The Girl who was Stolen from

Do you even feel regret
For the moment you wrongfully took
Was your pleasure worth the pain and tears I drowned in?
Something I'll always relive
But can simply never be given back
I trembled in fear that day and years following just that
Do you even care? No
Do you know the monster you are? Maybe
You stole, like from a child,
But still no repercussion
If there is one thing I learned
It's that by using my voice
I can help those who are stolen from
And make thieves feel worse
I can prevent these awful moments
And the gory nauseas details
But I will never live in fear
Even when your presence is unknown

Company

Company would be nice
The sight of someone else
Would help my heart slow
And help my brain know
I'm scared but okay though

Company would be nice
One touch of skin to mine
Reaching for the fear in sight
Making it disappear all night
Covering my eyes when there's light

Company would be nice
Because if you were here
When the nightmares recur
Your presence ensures
It I will no longer endure

Relive

I'm tired and I keep crying
Crying over what I use to have
Have a life full of good and not bad
Bad things now seem to follow me
Me and my demons we are tied too
Too many drinks to sleep again
Again I just wait for it to all end
End this torment my body is in
In this moment I wish most to be free
Free my brain from constant thinking
Thinking of how I'm tired and I keep crying

Train of Thought

I speak but my words mean nothing
There is fog all in my mind
My train of thought is late
And frankly it has been behind
I'm tired of the brain confusion
Although this enemy is not new
With no rest, you'll be in slow motion
No sleep will do it to you too

Death's Case

The life she was provided was so unfair
Lies, crime, neglect, addiction in the air
All her life she was repeatedly betrayed
By the system, men, family and the price she paid

She was innocent, little, she didn't deserve it
"Just lay low, say yes, and always submit"
No support, no help, no one in their right mind
She prayed at night for a resolution to find

For a little she walked in the path she was shown
Abuse and neglect was all she had known
Sold herself until she had no one to be
And one day she wept, "I will do better for the baby in me"

She walked through hell, but found the door
She began to wonder, "is life worth living for?"
For once she saw a glimpse of hope in sight
She said to herself, "I just have to make it through the night"

She ran off the path, though obstacles were there
"I promise you won't know this path, I swear"
She worked the worst jobs, long nights, and hours
Hoping one day she'll be on the path with flowers

She didn't stop there she did inner work too
And learned the patterns and traumas she never knew
She was providing, happier in the right pace
She is finally living, and out of death's case

Head or Heart

Constantly at war with head or heart
Do I follow feelings or logic, not sure where to start
Following feelings is like walking down a slope
It's difficult to stop
You get pushed faster by hope

Following logic seems the right thing to do
The path appears clear to me
But it definitely hurts you

Maybe the answer is I can choose both
And cross over by bridge
And have my own growth

My Old Self

I found the girl I was looking for
The happy one from my past
She isn't ashamed of her passions
And she loves the world she's in

She surrounds herself with people
Because people are what she loves
She allows tests to try her
And she passes them all too

I love how she smiles again
And it brings good tears to her eyes
Because there was a time I didn't think
I'd be my old self again

PART 2 : LOVE AND LOSS

Comfort

Comfort, my home and my friend
The place where I know I belong
My love for you Comfort won't come to an end
You are every breath, morning, and song

There is not a day where Comfort is not by my side
Sleep together, live together, dream, and laugh
In your arms and words I completely abide,
For I know with you Comfort, is my other half

Comfort can be found anywhere, but you hold that name
Comfort brings me joy and accepts my shame

Drowning

Water under my feet
not worried about the time
It reminds me of the beach
Looking at new waves I'm

Noticing water at my ankles
Reminds me of being a kid
Like jumping in the puddles
Scared to get wet but did

The water is to my hips
Like the moment in the pool
Ignoring everything else
Yet thirsting for a cool

The water is to my head now
How come I never knew
That drowning was so easy
Was my distraction you

Mirage

This whole thing was a mirage
Confusion surrounds my ears
My heart is sifting out the pain
There's anger in my tears

I give more than even asked
You were so fresh anew
How do I stop stretching me
I'm stained with faded hue

I liked being home this time
I had comfort in my own skin
Anxiety pouring out my eyes
Where did the bluffs begin

Emotions, touch, invisible
Ends black like they all do
The depressing motive of your words
Was to lay at night with you

The Sun and the Cloud

The sun gave a chance to the cloud
But all he did was dim her shine
He promised to give her love
But rarely let her see the world
One day he brought her rain
And sun thought she was dying
She shooed the cloud away
So she could shimmer again

I Hate My Head

I hate my head sometimes because it confuses me
Memories drown out the logic and lust floods out the pain
My dreams they are some me but some are merely hope
Even when I go days, weeks, and months you always seem to linger
Like a curse put on me by God telling me to help your soul
My thoughts of you are full of disgust but I can't help but smile
You anger me in ways I can't even comprehend
The fear of seeing you aches all the time in my head
I hate that I long for your touch and your tight embrace
But in the end I hate my head because in it you hold your place

Devalued

You don't see behind the makeup
Blue eyes and all the hair
You say "what a pretty face"
And you're caught up in what I wear
Your sight stops at the surface
You think I don't have any thoughts
But we both know you surely do
Of those opinions, you have lots
I know someone taught you this
although it's hard for you to recall
That all women, and I included
Are more than objects after all

My Flaws to You

I am too nice
I hold my head high
I don't shed a tear
I don't throw people under the bus
And I try to keep a secret
I won't betray you because I am loyal
I know my own worth and I know what I deserve
I am the bigger person
I won't bash you when I know all your secrets
I won't bring up the wrongs you've done to me
I forgive and give multiple chances
I learn my lessons and I say yes too often
I don't give myself credit I deserve
I always strive to see the good in others
I know I have a beautiful soul
But I don't always think I'm beautiful
I try to be true to myself but sometimes I fail
I put too much faith in others who haven't earned it
I am annoying at times but happy when I'm laughing
I love being around people that get me

Vow

Write me letters
Small ones
Not anything too crazy

Be there
when I'm sad
And in happy times too

Look at me
With those brown eyes
Like the first time you did

Kiss me
With love
And there will be peace

Remember me
When distant
And away for a while

Tell me
Dumb stuff
And I'll promise to laugh

Know me
Deeply
And you'll fall in love every day

Keep me
In your heart
And away from trouble too

To Love You or To Love Me

When I imagine it all, I see you,
But I don't think I'm in your debut
You say the right things but don't follow through
My issues with you just grew

But if you were here, would you still stay
Or would all your promises fade away
I'm collecting lies like an ashtray
I feel like I am just your prey

In the end I think I can do better
But I don't know why I won't let her
Do I let this cycle recur
My desired answer is a blur

If I follow my heart, I will grow frail
Thinking with my head would be the right trail
To love you and allow myself to fail
Or to love me and only prevail

A Flirt

You laugh and I smile
Then we do it all again
I'll want to stay for a while
Cause you aren't like them

That twinkle in your eye
Says all that I need to know
We both give out a sigh
When we realize it's late and time to go

But when you flirt it's cute
I feel it's just us in this place
There's no one better you suit
You never cease to put a smile on my face

But flirting is just simple
It's short, and it's sweet
The concept is so peaceful
And the joy is my treat

Soul Crusher

I was limp not able to walk
You shoved me down and stomped
I was mute four days or five
Not a tear or word in sight

I was frozen in the ice
Heart stopped beating, numb was nice
You tried thawing out my pity
But I already died that day

I was covering my ears
Locked my heart up with my tears

Nightmares

It's interesting how someone can be human
Then change to not human at all
To not give a care or call
When the person they loved is hurting

But are you having nightmares like me
The inability to sleep
Do you also fear for your life
When you lay your head at night

Are you having flashbacks too
Of a night so horrible and blue
I'm stained with a permanent hue
And you just get to go back to, your life

And the saddest part of me
Is when I'm crying and dying
All I ever want to do
Is to reach out and ask you

To rescue me, but I forgot
All your feelings left that day when you did
And I left your mind in an instant
Never to return again

You forgot me like I was a blink
A moment in the unnecessary wind
A rock in your shoe you removed
Finally, you're free, you must be so happy

(continued on the back)

And this isn't about you,
Or wanting you back cause I don't
It's about me having no one to keep me safe
And remembering you did as hope

I thought if I said the word you'd be knocking at my door
I just need a rescuer someone to cover my ears at night
Hold me a little closer
And be with me through the fight

But tonight, I have medication
Yes, I drug myself to sleep
And some nights it gives me nightmares too
But it's the only way I'll count sheep

Fireworks

That night we saw fireworks in all types of ways
When you pushed my hair behind my ear and gave me that
brown eyed gaze

A match was struck when you and I sat and talked for hours
The wick was lit never to end, catching up was like fresh flowers

The tension between us was thrilling and waiting to explode
The sparks they flew everywhere when our true colors showed

This is not the end for there is never just one display
But next time when I see your face, I will not know what to say

Maybe I wasn't Meant to Love

Maybe I wasn't meant to love
Because I always love too hard
And I end up leaving more scarred
Then the other person will anyway

Maybe I wasn't meant to love
Because I'm dying giving my all
I held them but they still let me fall
From stories and stories and don't care

Maybe I wasn't meant to love
Because I'll never get what I can give
And yet I always have to relive
That I was the only one who meant it

Maybe I wasn't meant to love
Because I'll be happier if I stop trying
My effort I can finally stop supplying
For people who will be gone in months

In Your Eyes

In your eyes I saw my future and I felt peace
The deep brown that held my soul
In my mind I still see your face and forehead crease
When I'm there I know I'm whole

I drown in your deep eyes and see it all
We both know my heart you stole
No returns, I will never send for a recall
The first one I issued my love to, you got the role

Beautiful Rain

Love came in the summer, love is rain
Unexpected, made my plans change
No umbrella no cover, just me and the rain

Washed away the hair, makeup, and all
Embraced the wet, the cold, and the raw

I became use to the daily rain
And when the rain ended, I noticed a pain
I'm dried out now, the nourishment was insane
I've always enjoyed standing in the rain

Let me

Let me know you fully
Trust me with the deep
Have I not been reliable
You know the inner me

Show me the soul naked
If not we'll stay still
Pride is a form of weakness
Cry with me and heal

There's safety in my comfort
No judgment for your past
Naturally I make bricks crumble
Just ask anyone from last

I'm not sorry I'm intuitive
It's a beauty of a thing
Most men can't accept it
But will you do it for me

I Stayed

You left
But I stayed
In the moment
Where all the love was

I stayed in the feelings of
Our first kiss, first dance
It was wonderful
I stayed hearing your laugh
In my dreams
It was so simple

I stayed in the good times
and the bad
But now I tell myself it was all good
And I tell myself it isn't over

Unfair

I've never begged someone to stay
Until it ended with you
Our cards dealt were so unfair
I've just lost my love, I have no air

Depression sucked every ounce of life
I hate what it did to you
I hear you saying you still love me
And I still love you too

Why I'll Always Love You

It's your laugh every time
And your big brown eyes
It's the messy hair, room, and heart
The way you look at me like I'm art

The best eye contact of my life
A sacred life in delight
The trust for you to be mine
For my very first time

The softness in your voice
"Honey" made me melt inside
The way you held me when I cried
Telling me "don't apologize"

You always understood me
Without having to speak a word
The one who made me feel like me
In love with you forever I'll be

Heartbreak Cuts

I already missed you before you were gone
And now I miss you more
Days without you are agony
They make my heart sore

I long for your presence, touch, embrace
Your smile was warmer than the sun
Your body kept me warm
Until there was the storm

It was such a tragedy when it crashed
No one to blame at all
But hurt surrounded each of us
A deep cut it did install

With Me and You

Cold toes
But with you they were warmer
Lame jokes
But with you they brought laughter
Insecurities
But with you they were strengths
Lonely life
But with you it became heaven

Long hair
But with me it got shorter
Loud times
But with me they were louder
Past mistakes
But with me they were just human
Feelings
But with me they were safe

Flowers

Flowers aren't too much to ask for
And neither is your attention
The moment when I learned that
Was my biggest lesson
I gave you every emotion
And you built walls so high
Someone will give their all to me
Once you've said goodbye
I know what I deserve now
Maybe it could have been you
If you'd only noticed
I was slipping away too

With You

I was the one who held it all together
And now you hold me
I carried the burdens of every other
Now I don't carry it alone

I'd cry in the shower and let the tears fall
But you catch every one I shed
I thought less of myself after them all
With you I adore the mirror more

And with you the days they last forever
Although I want to count down the time
To have you fully, what would be clever
To encase your heart with all of mine

Let's do the Things You Never Do

Let's do the things you never do
Singing out loud to ever song
See me every day all week long
Meeting family or a few
Let's do the things you never do

Let's see the places no one sees
Actions that give me the stability
Showing your heart and vulnerability
You make this all such a breeze
Showing me places no one sees

I'll give you things you never got
The person who wants you for you
Tears, laughs, and all we go through
Someone who appreciates you a lot
I'll give you the things you never got

Let's have the moments all the time
Of staring in each other's eyes
Making one laugh after cries
This thing is worth the climb
So let's have these moments all the time

Now let me look at you again
You bring peace to me in every glance
I never thought I'd have a chance
To be with one of the best men
Now let me look at you again
Now let's do the thing you never do
Like spending a very long time with you

Selfish

I laugh at all the times I should've left you and cursed
Maybe then I'd find the knife you used
To stab me in the back first
All the decisions were about you, you never cared for me
But everything that I showed you was in sincerity

I must take a crumb of ownership
I should have knocked you out
Of my life and not looked back even with your tears and pout
I often sit and hope you drown, you are a selfish twit
Drown in the impact of your decisions and go to hell for it
I don't want you to feel special thinking I wrote this just for you
Because can't you clearly see this is for your selfish friends too

A Spark

It's the spark that shows me that this will be good
The comfort that proves it's all worth it
I love the feeling of where we are and where we stood
So close, intertwined like we are knit

It's always me in the room you seem to find
No shame or desire to even hide it
Your face perks up like I'm a breath of air, so kind
Our touch means so much even though we won't admit

I love how you always say I'm the reason you came
The comfort is real it's like no one else is there
There isn't even point in confession because you feel the same
And without each other our souls are bare

Music

The worst thing about music
Is how I connected it with you
That song that was my all
I can't bear to listen to

When I hear it I see your face
And us laughing in the car
But I'd rather play something strange
So my feelings can go far

Call it what you want
But I'll call it my separation
From the moments that we shared
Keeping my heart's preservation

PART 3 : EXCERPTS OF LIFE

I am Woman

I fight to have a say
I fight to be beautiful
I fight to be loved
I fight for my rights
I fight for my voice to be heard over men
I fight to not "overreact"
I fight for my friends
I fight for my children
I fight for my space
I fight not to be prude
I fight for my family
I fight my own mental battles
I fight postpartum depression
I fight for my safety
I fight for my story to be believed
I fight for equal pay
I fight for my position
I fight for my life

Today I fought and tomorrow I fight again
Didn't they tell you; this is life as a woman

The Painter

Some people paint our portraits
And the image they want to see
But somehow it doesn't look right
In fact, I'm thinking what is that
Does that really look like me
But the artist just keeps going
There's colors I'd never use
This thing looks so horrible
No way am I their muse
In life I've learned one big lesson
I must take the brush from their hand
Because I am also an artist
The end I need to demand
My portrait won't meet their expectations
In fact it won't even look close
This artist will paint how I feel
who I am and it will look like me the most
Some people paint our portraits
Of who they want us to be
And if you don't take the brush away
Their goals and expectations of you
in your portrait will always be

Growing Up

Once we were just girls who played dress up and all
Makeovers, sleepovers, and too often at the mall
I think back to the days riding horses and letting go
Crying over boys and dumb fights that teens often know
But I came all this way to see you today
I am so happy for you, it feels like my big day
I think back to the days when we were just four and five
And now that we're here I can't help but cry
I'm seeing you stand there in that all white dress
I can't help but get sentimental, we're both a mess
To talk to your parents and reminisce from the past
I'm sorry it's been so long since I saw them last
But today is a day of cheer, memories, and guests
To see you so happy and in love is the best
You deserve the love you always showed to others
So I'll raise up my glass and cheer to new lovers

Parental Guidance

Have good friends
Eat your peas
Make good grades
Don't drink please

Graduate and
Don't do drugs
The are the things
The parents love

Work real hard
Marry well
Make good money
Pray, no hell

You did it all
But still I say
I'm not impressed
By you today

Look what they do
Oh I adore
You accomplished all
But please do more

Childlike

Pure heart, soul, and body
naïve to the things of the world

I miss that girl

She played with toys, not with feelings
Cried over physical pain and not emotional pain
Loved her body because she didn't know how to compare it
Didn't worry about money or making ends meet
But worried about what friend she would see that day
She hadn't experienced heartbreak and wasn't scared of it
She used her voice and didn't care what others would think

But then she got older, and life got harder
She learned a lot from society, people, and loss
And all she wanted to do was be that little girl again

The Artist

A person with a lot going on and nothing at all
He is brave, bold, and holds his pride tall

He's just a soul to care so deeply for
His pretty mask is one that all adore

But there's more to this boy than just a pretty face
I often know that he feels out of place

With the experiences of the world held in his hand
He gives out a bright glow, a fresh taste, a new brand

The deeper you go the more the shell
But I'm glad I've got to know him so well

He can truly make me laugh any time of day
I pray our friendship may never fall away

Sometimes there's a mystery I see in him still
But I love how his depth can give me a chill

With him there's always a story and tale
He tries but with me I see straight through his veil

Although I disagree with some of his decisions
I watch him create some incredible visions

I hope his joy and passion never fade
Because I'm always in awe at everything he's made

I love this boy with all my heart
I'm so glad he's my piece of art

Because of You

You ask me why haven't I moved on
Because you never taught me how to
You ask me why can't I stop crying
Because you never taught me how to
You ask why I can't process my trauma
Because you never taught me how to
You ask why am I not telling you things
Because you never taught me how to
You ask why I'm not being honest with you
Because you never taught me how to
You ask why am I taking a break
Because you never taught me how to
You ask why can't you be happy with your life
Because you never taught me how to
You ask why don't you find real love
Because you never taught me how to

How To Be Me

When I was younger, I wondered how to be me
Is it morals I grew up with that will help me from wondering
Is it the people I met in college or work that will help me see
Is it my interests, talents, body, or brain, please guide me

Lost in a sea of people I could become
But I don't want to mess up be stupid or dumb
What if I don't like the person I am
Can I switch like an outfit to a different woman

I think I know at times, I mean I'm loyal and true
But sometimes others don't hold these of value
I think I am me most when I'm happy
I'm glad I know who I am now, this is sappy

The Dove

She was a dove of a person known for pure heart and peace
And always tried to care for those she would meet

Kindness follows her but she worked hard, she earned it
A beautiful soul though she would never think to admit

Trying her best to learn and to grow
Helping others are the seeds she'll sew

A dove was a symbol God used and God uses her too
To restore hearts of people and show they have value

The First

To figure it all out first was her role
It's seemed very hard, a burden of a toll

She still conquered every challenge she met
Stubborn and firm her mind always set

A joy fills the room when she is inside
I love how she grows and with me she'll confide

Creating and journeys follow her still
She's the first born and has very strong will

P. S.

Yellow roses and a sea by me
Those are the thing I love so dearly
Go to Irish lands, hear songs sung too
These are the things I long to do

Explore the world, adventure is on my side
And with my sisters I will abide
We'll have stories to tell at every place
And pictures to pose with smiling face

An army man who loved so much
Father, husband sweet with every touch
For in the past I said goodbye
And forever in love with him I'm tied

My family is fun, it's crazy and wild
But when all together my heart has a smile
Every moment with them is one I hold dearly
And the love we have is one I feel clearly

The Sea of Friendship

To care for everyone but no one care for me
Is like a sailboat alone, lost at sea

Once the sun sets it's frigid and cold
Much like needing someone but no one's there to hold

The boats will pass and stop to see
"what do you have that will benefit me"

It's hard to locate the shore at times
Just like it is a loyal friend to confide

But when you do find friends that are true
It's just like treasure something of great value

Savior

God, you saved me from those moments
I never thought I'd know
You held my hand so tight
When I was dying and felt alone
You brought angels to me in time of need
And that was no mistake
They helped put me back together
And didn't let me re-break

Woman in Hiding

There is a woman I often see
Who appears to be trapped in her own body
She hides her opinions and beliefs
And allows her emotions to fall off like leaves

If you saw her too you'd never guess
Her smile is bright her hair is fresh
If you see her enough, some days you'll find
The secretive woman who is trapped inside

There are rare moments I observed, only a few
I learned her personal things I never knew
A glimpse of the damsel who hides from all
She worries if she comes out, like leaves she'll fall

One day I hope I see her for longer
As she gets older her chance of escape is stronger
Because how long can one hide behind an image of perfection
And live in fear of everyone else's rejection

But the woman who hides is the prettiest of all
She's gracious, forgiving, the one I'd call
She doesn't know if she showed, people would love her more
There's beauty in the brokenness and pain from her war

Dreams

The dreams I keep having will never end
I want to say they are blissful but torture is their friend
My dreams are hours and thriving on detail
A glimpse of what I want but when I wake they fail
Love so pure and a touch so sweet
These are the dreams I will never meet
It seems so real and is so true
Yet I wake each morning anew
I hate every minute of being awake
Because the dreams are so perfect for my soul's sake
I wish I could dream and never arise
But these dreams aren't real only head lies

So what do I do each night you ask
I close my eyes, in the dreams I bask

In a Jar

Some people live life trapped in a jar
They're in a small space and won't go too far
They're happy in their spot, I mean, it's glass they can see
Everything around them and who they'd never be
They judge in their jar, because why would they worry
Their jar was made right it's tough and it's sturdy
They see when life strikes the ones not in the jar
And think "that sucks" I can't believe you scar
They can never relate, empathize, or understand
I mean they're still in their jar just like they planned
Not worried about others on the outside they see
Thinking "oh heavens! I'm glad that's not me"
But slowly the others will crack their safe jars
They'll experience the world learning how it is ours
Because if you live your life in a bubble
You'll never see your own selfishness as trouble

Beautiful Girl

Beautiful girl you are worth so much
Your words are like songs
You love in your touch

Beautiful girl you are so strong
You should forgive yourself
Even when you're wrong

Beautiful girl mistakes are okay
You can start over tomorrow
It will be a new day

Beautiful girl you are so kind
As peaceful as nature
Let's get out of our mind

Beautiful girl you are not alone
Just look a little harder
With love you're sown

Beautiful girl you are a treasure
Comparison doesn't matter
Beauty has no measure

Beautiful girl I hope you never forget
Read this when you're stuck
And your strength will reset

She's a Gem

When I see her, I'm reminded of my younger self
When I just wanted someone to love me
With innocent pure mind only seeing good in people
She is easily hurt yet wouldn't hurt another soul
She can't handle conflict and it's so hard to say no
That's why I like her, she is sweet
She sits in other's shadows but wants to be chosen first
And she deserves to be, but they are intimidated by her purity
Because they don't want to taint her
I hope she never experiences real heartbreak
I don't want her sparkle to not shine
I want to wrap her in a cocoon
And only let her have the best
Because her soul is more special than the rest

What Women Want

Freedom to choose what I think is right
Receiving the credit for ideas I had
Excitement to go to places at night
No fear of what will happen if he's mad

Laugh in a park with our friends, no care
Go to gas up and not get approached for once
Freely in public, no fear to bare
Exercising with others without sexual hunts

Dressing for myself and not getting scolded
No opinions of my shape just love and support
No pressure to fit the perfect image that's molded
Not having to fight for our truth in court

Others actually know how our bodies function
And the hormones, cramps, and pain we see
The care about women is not a production
Where rest after birth is a guarantee

To not lock the door immediately after
No one to yell at me their sexual slurs
Not contemplating if I can run faster
I won't have to teach my daughter safety's not hers

Outgrew

I was planted by you
But I never stopped there
Took my time to lay good ground
Knowing it was important

Like spring it came fast
And I soared into the sky
Growing taller and taller
Until I realized

I outgrew you
You stayed planted in the ground
And I've been watered by many
Life experiences and goals around

I outgrew you
By learning how to be a good support
And discovering how you won't
When I was in season of drought

I outgrew you
Because I became strong
Instead of falling for something easy
And playing the patterns again

I outgrew you
And I don't judge you for that
But you're held down by weeds
And I just can't hold back

Soulmate

She is my soul she is my one
Understanding me forever
When I hold the moon she brings the sun
Her help is always clever

No one ever will compare
Her love is holding me
Her presence is always light, it's air
Lets my authentic be

We are a knot, and we are tied
Connections like this are few
As life moves, with her I ride
Cause friends are soulmates too

ABOUT THE AUTHOR

I began writing poetry when I was an adolescent. Since then, I have had many life experiences which have caused me deep emotions. Writing poetry and journaling would help me navigate those experiences. Writing poetry became more than a way to acknowledge my emotions, but a hobby and way to tell the stories and struggles of those around me. Additionally, I have obtained a bachelor's degree in psychology and a masters in mental health counseling. Many of my poems are related to my own mental health experiences or just from the lens of a therapist. I wanted to include mental health into my poetry because it is a big part of who I am and what I'm passionate about. I also want to allow others to see that you can sit in the space of your emotions. Acknowledging and feeling those feelings is part of healing and being human. This poetry means a lot to me, it feels like you're holding a piece of my soul. My hope in allowing other people to read my poetry, is that people connect to it and know they are not alone. You are not alone.

Made in the USA
Coppell, TX
05 April 2025

47867887R00111